SURVIVE OR THRIVE?
WORKBOOK

A Guide to Creating
THE LIFE YOU WANT
Out of
THE LIFE YOU HAVE

Survive or Thrive Workbook
Step by step workbook to help you solve life problems and thrive again

iUniverse books may be ordered through booksellers or by contacting:

iUniverse
1663 Liberty Drive
Bloomington, IN 47403
www.iuniverse.com
1-800-Authors (1-800-288-4677)

ISBN: 978-1-4620-8403-6 (sc)
ISBN: 978-1-4620-8404-3 (e)

Printed in the United States of America

iUniverse rev. date: 1/5/2011

SURVIVE OR THRIVE?

Creating THE LIFE YOU WANT Out of THE LIFE YOU HAVE

Stepp Stevens Sydnor
with Suzi Streit

Stepp Stevens Sydnor

Stepp Stevens Sydnor is a multi-talented speaker, author, radio personality, and business owner with twenty-four years of experience in his genre.

He started his professional career in electronic sales and transitioned into owning a retail company, which he grew into seven retail stores, two manufacturing plants, and ninety employees. Although he is naturally gifted, Stepp gained exponential corporate development skills from this experience. After selling his business, Stepp continued to widen his knowledge and skill set by working for various technology business owners performing sales and marketing.

Stepp is a self-starter who emphasizes learning new things, and fuses his acquired "street smarts" from past experiences into his teaching and concepts. The synergy between his business experiences and his understanding of human behavior has brought a uniquely integrated perspective to his business and his coaching.

In 1999, Stepp founded The TurnAround Group, now TurnAround Training Solutions, LLC, to assist companies in improving their profitability by focusing on leadership and sales performance. He has developed nine training seminars, as well as coaching and mentoring programs in the areas of sales, leadership, culture, personal development, and stress management. Stepp's clients have ranged from public-sector organizations such as PricewaterhouseCoopers and Dallas Housing Authority to industry leaders such as Cox Communications, Sam's Club, Time Warner Cable, Brookshires and Robroy Industries.

He continued to diversify his talent with the release of his book *Survive or Thrive?* in 2008. Stepp plans to also accomplish new and grander goals including authoring other successful books on topics such as managing life, and making money through sales.

Stepp grew up in Richardson, Texas, and currently resides in Whitehouse, Texas. He is the father of three teenagers.

Acknowledgements

It took a few years to get this workbook finished, but at last, here it is. There are so many "propellers" that have shaped my life and purpose, and to all of you I am so thankful. I want to express my heartfelt gratitude to all those who have helped me see the difference between surviving and thriving with greater clarity. To Suzi Streit, my good friend and writer who helped me to stay focused and organized, whose ideas and editing helped shape this workbook. To Karen Dodd, for gentle patience with lost receipts (like socks in a dryer they just disappear), constant attention to details, and encouraging smile. To Kim Beckham, who sparked the fire for the Survive or Thrive? topic and continues to sharpen my ideas. To Randy Stevenson, who is a constant encourager and motivator. To Lea Rittenhouse, for editing, reading, and organizing the material to make better sense to the publisher. To my kids Nick Sydnor, Nicole Sydnor, and Joshua Sydnor, for just always being there. And to my brother Rick Sydnor, who is truly a best friend. Also, special thanks to my sister Bobbie Woods for cheering me on, and to Lisa Susan Robertson for her patience, prayers, and hours of listening to me talk about this project. I am blessed with wonderful friends and colleagues—and an amazing abundance of love.

Contents

Introduction

How do you handle life problems and challenges?

In today's world, we are expected to push through all kinds of adversity, and arrive at our destination with a smile on our face and a positive attitude. But, what do you do when your efforts, intentions, hopes, dreams, expectations, plans, and visions simply do not turn out the way you expected?

Change happens to everyone, and in a moment, your world can be turned upside down.

Consider these questions...

Do you know anyone who has gone through significant change in the last six months?

Is there someone close to you who has gone through significant change in the last six months?

Have you gone, or are you currently going through a significant change in the last six months?

This workbook, along with the *Survive or Thrive book* invites you on an adventure to re-think HOW you deal with:

- Life's ups and downs
- False perceptions and realities
- Unbalanced emotions
- Hardships and disappointments
- Change and pressure
- Fear and anxiety
- Loss of hope
- Negative thoughts and thinking patterns
- Unsuccessful behavior patterns
- Feelings of uncertainty and doubt

Right now, you may be struggling to survive a bitter blow resembling a failed relationship or business, financial challenges, job loss, or perhaps the death of a dream or loved one. You might be swept away in the emotions the hardships of life accompany including but not limited to: shock, fear, loneliness, and desperation.

If you're going through a difficult time and are unsure of your future, know that you're in good company, the company of every person on earth!

Everyone, at some time in their life, will face difficulties.

The focus of this workbook is the different styles of thinking we can use to push through life problems. One is called *SURVIVE thinking* involving natural instincts, the other is called *THRIVE thinking* defined as recognizing you have choices. The most natural and completely normal course of handling life's problems is to SURVIVE them. However, this way of thinking is where many get stuck, and can never move out of survive mode to thrive mode.

Has Survive thinking been elevated to an art form?

Why? How?

What examples can you think of?

It's no wonder we think simply getting through each day is enough to ask for in life. We tend to stop at survival instead of taking the next step toward a new and more fulfilling existence. If we've faced trauma and tragedy, we may stay linked to our troubles, insisting we're fighting for our life long after the actual threat has passed.

We have a habit of holding onto our survival mentality, rather than using our hardships to heal and grow, and to help others learn from the lessons of our own experience.

This workbook is about moving from a survival mindset to a thriving one.

This workbook is about accomplishing more than simply surviving in this life by training yourself to rethink your situation, so you can create a better life.

It's your choice: *Survive or Thrive*?

The question is: Which option will YOU choose?

Think About It...

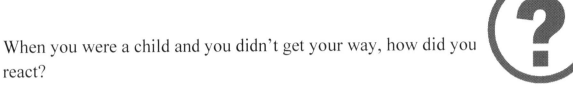

When you were a child and you didn't get your way, how did you react?

Where do you believe you learned to handle problems?

How did your parents handle life's problems?

How do these positive or negative patterns affect your thinking today?

Chapter One

Is Life Fair?

During a break at one of my company's seminars a woman asked me, "Do you think life is fair?" I was quick to answer, "No, it's certainly not." To my surprise she retorted, "I think it is. Sooner or later, it breaks everybody's heart." Later on that evening, I thought about what she had said and concluded that, in a way, she was right. I guess life is fair, because everyone will experience a level of hardship at some time. No one is immune to the knocks of life. Your family, money, religion, status, power, and position all shape who you are, but none of these elements can protect you from the storms of life.

> **"I, not events, have the power to make me happy or unhappy today.
> I can choose which it shall be."**
> *Groucho Marx*

"I have bad news."

A phone call similar to the one pictured above can change everything in your life in a matter of seconds. Change doesn't ask for permission. More often than not, it hits unexpectedly and out of the blue. One thing you can be sure of is change will happen. However, negative changes that happen do not determine our destiny. How you respond to life problems is what defines your future. You must learn the difference between what happens to you, and how you react.

Why? Because challenges come in all shapes and sizes.

Think About It....

What kind of changes/challenges do you deal with in your life?

Personal:

Professional:

Read the following story and answer the questions below.

A Perfect Picture of Peace[i]

Long ago a man sought the perfect picture of peace. Not finding one that satisfied, he announced a contest to produce this masterpiece. The challenge stirred the imagination of artists everywhere, and paintings arrived from far and wide.

Finally, the great day of revelation arrived. The judges uncovered one peaceful scene after another, while viewers clapped and cheered. The tension grew. Only two pictures remained veiled.

As a judge pulled the cover from one, a hush fell over the crowd. A mirror-smooth lake reflected lacy, green birches under the soft blush of the evening sky. Along the grassy shore, a flock of sheep grazed undisturbed. Surely this was the winner.

The man with the vision uncovered the second painting himself, and the crowd gasped in surprise. Could this be peace? A tumultuous waterfall cascaded down a rocky precipice; the crowd could almost feel its cold, penetrating spray. Stormy-grey clouds threatened to explode with lightening, wind and rain. In the midst of the thundering noises and bitter chill, a spindly tree clung to the rocks at the edge of the falls. One of its branches reached out in front of the torrential waters as if foolishly seeking to experience its full power. A little bird had built a nest in the elbow of that branch. Content and undisturbed in her stormy surroundings, she rested on her eggs. With her eyes closed and her wings ready to cover her little ones, she manifested peace that transcends all earthly turmoil.

What does this story mean to you?

How can you apply it to the situations in your life?

Chapter Two
Managing Our Self-Talk

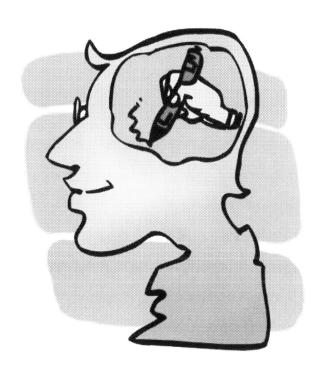

As we go through life, everything we see, hear, and experience causes us to draw a conclusion about what is taking place on around us. "Self-talk" is *our* interpretation of what *we think* happened. For instance, assume your spouse comes home, walks right by you as he or she enters the house, and responds to your "Hi, honey" with a grunt and a half-hearted wave. You tell yourself, "My spouse is obviously upset with me. It must be because I worked late last night. He/she is so self-centered. I didn't even enjoy working late. What a jerk!"

If this was the story you were telling yourself about your spouse, what kinds of feelings would you have toward your spouse?

Would these feelings affect your behavior? How?

Imagine you pass by your boss in a hallway and say hello. He or she ignores you and says nothing. This isn't the way your boss normally responds to you, but lately the company hasn't been doing very well, and there is talk of cutting costs.

What are you thinking?

How are you feeling?

Our emotions don't just happen. We actually create them. The "self-talk" going on within us gives birth to our emotions. Once our emotions kick in, they become our primary focus. Emotions motivate our behavior, and when we are emotional we aren't logical.

Why do you believe this is true?

What are the consequences of thinking this way?

Our self-talk is very powerful as illustrated in the chart below.

Negative Self-Talk →	**Negative Feelings** →	***Negative Actions***

Positive Self-Talk →	**Positive Feelings** →	***Positive Actions***

Neutral Self-Talk →	**Controlled Feelings** →	***Logical Actions***

If we are going to stay logical and effective, we must be able to manage our "self talk." The first step toward managing our self-talk is realizing that what we tell ourselves is often more fictional or opinion rather than fact. Once we develop "self-talk" in our mind, we often do not question it—we accept it, believe it, and becomes fact in our minds. Negative stories create negative emotions, which lead to negative actions. From every set of facts, there can be an infinite number of stories. To manage our self-talk, we need to tell ourselves a different story and focus on more positive self-talk. We can change our self-talk by separating the facts from the story. When we make this separation, we can look at the events in our lives with unbiased observation.

What is a fact? A fact is something we can verify or prove. A fictional story is simply our opinion or a judgment of the facts. An opinion cannot be proven or verified. Facts can be proven and verified if they are true.

Fact or Fiction?

Are the following statements fact or a fictional story? Circle the correct answer.

1.	"I was laid off from my job."	Fact	Fiction
2.	"Management is out to get me."	Fact	Fiction
3.	"My husband's Visa bill has an unknown hotel on it."	Fact	Fiction
4.	"My son is going be a failure at college and isn't mature enough to leave home."	Fact	Fiction
5.	"I was laid off work because they don't like me."	Fact	Fiction
6.	"My co-worker isn't a team player."	Fact	Fiction
7.	"I don't have any talents—I must be bad at everything."	Fact	Fiction
8.	"I got a low performance review."	Fact	Fiction
9.	"My husband is having an affair."	Fact	Fiction
10.	"My son failed a class."	Fact	Fiction
11.	"My boss doesn't like me."	Fact	Fiction
12.	"I wasn't picked for the soccer team."	Fact	Fiction

Answers on page 64

Separating the Facts from Fiction in Your Life

The fictional self-talk stories you tell yourself keep you stuck in survival mode. They validate the idea that the best you can do is simply get by. Think about the greatest challenge you face right now. In the space below, begin writing your story—complete with all the drama and emotion you feel about the events that have happened. Don't hold back, let it all out.

My story:

Now look at what you have written and ask:

What am I telling myself—positive or negative—about what has happened?

What is the worst that can happen?

What is the best?

Am I acting like the worst will happen to me or the best?

Now, make a list of the facts of your event, without any story, drama or judgment.

FACTS:

1.

2.

3.

4.

5.

Read and reflect on your list of facts and ask yourself:

Is this a fact or fiction?

What self-talk stories am I creating?

What other story could there be based on these facts?

"When you change the way you look at things, the things you look at change."
Author Unknown

Chapter Three

The Difference between Surviving and Thriving

Life-altering challenges plunge us into survival mode. This is normal and necessary. Survival is the first phase of recovery, and is good! But, it's meant to be a beginning point not to an end. The following events are examples of life situations that could plunge people into survival.

- John and Ann are awakened by a call from the police telling them their teen-age son has been killed in a car accident.
- Tammy has been under a lot of pressure from her job. Yesterday her boss sent her an email placing more responsibility on her. She doesn't think she can take the pressure, it's just too much.
- Danny knew he was spending more than his income would allow. Now the debt is so large that all his money goes to pay interest.
- Karen, Steve and their children are homeless. A tornado ripped apart their neighborhood.
- Joanne tells her executive team that the company is going to make drastic cuts and that their survival is on the line.
- Jodie and Robert's daughter tells them a church staff member has been molesting her.
- Lily sits in shock as she hears the news that the plant she works at is closing in 30 days.
- Angie finds out she has stage-four cancer.

- Rebecca's husband tells her he is unhappy and wants a divorce.

- Bill sees no alternate options for his company other than filing bankruptcy.

Think about challenges you see people experience and list them here.

1.

2.

3.

4.

5.

6.

What kind of behaviors do you see in people when they experience challenges like these? Brainstorm and list as many different behaviors as you can imagine.

1.

2.

3.

4.

5.

6.

Look at the list of behaviors you made on the previous page. Would you classify them as survive behaviors or thrive behaviors? Why? List them in the appropriate column below.

Survive Behaviors	Thrive Behaviors

Thrivers:

- Bounce back better than before

- Have a kind of super-resilience

- Feel fear, but choose to have courage

- Focus on capabilities and not excuses

Survivors:

- Feel that life happens *to* them

- Believe that the best they can do is dodge bullets and put out fires

- Blame others

- Feel helpless

Survivors and thrivers behave in distinct opposing ways as illustrated in the chart on the next page. One behavior exhibits specific characteristics of a survivor, and the other behavior describes a thriver's positive characteristics. The purpose of these survivor-thriver characteristics is to help you see where you are in life. Thriving is a choice, and to make that choice you have to have the ability to identify the behaviors. This chart will help you recognize where you are, and what adjustments you need to make to move toward creating the life you want!

"Life is what we make it. Always has been, always will be."
Grandma Moses

Think of a challenge you're dealing with then look at the behaviors on the chart. Circle the behaviors you see in yourself as you deal with this situation.

Surviving		_Thriving_
1. **Self-Preservation**	vs.	**Self-Growth**
Shocked		Healing
Withdrawn		Engaged
Helpless		Empowered
2. **Victim**	vs.	**Warrior**
Blaming		Accountable
Hopeless		Determined
Emotional		Logical
3. **Parasite**	vs.	**Player**
Passive		Assertive
Energy-absorbing		Energy-producing
Reactive		Proactive
4. **Actor**	vs.	**Director**
Can't be done		Can be done
Present-focused		Future-focused
Unclear identity		Clear identity

Do you see more behaviors in the thriving column or the surviving column?

Carrots, Eggs and Coffee Beans *(author unknown)*

Just as different foods respond differently in hot water, the same can be said of people. What happens when you put carrots in a pot of boiling water? How about eggs or coffee beans? When we fill three pots with water—put carrots in the first, eggs in the second, and coffee beans in the third—then turn up the heat, we see that different things happen. The carrots go in strong and hard but soften when they're boiled. The eggs stay hard on the outside, but their soft insides stiffen. Yet the coffee beans don't change their form or texture. Instead, they release a part of themselves to change their surroundings—filling the water and the air with their essence.

Let's face it. Painful personal trauma and tragedy—like illness or injury, death of a loved one, loss of a job, or the unexpected breakup of a relationship—are unavoidable. The question is: will these private calamities erode our capacity to be happy or cause us to become stronger and better able to live a meaningful and fulfilling life?

Some people start out with strength like the carrots but wilt in the face of adversity. When faced with a loss or other trial, the Survivor's spirit is like the inside of an egg: hardship "hard boils" their heart. Others are coffee beans, infusing the world with their inner richness when the heat is on.

Ask yourself: *How do I respond when I'm in hot water? Am I a carrot, an egg, or a coffee bean?*

Chapter Four
Self-Preservation Versus Self-Growth

Self-Preservation

Protecting from harm and danger – natural survival technique

When we are in shock, we freeze. Our instinct is survival, and at times, it seems like only way to survive is to pull into our shell and protect ourselves from all harm and danger. This is often exactly what we need in the beginning. It's an important stage in healing, but the danger is pulling into our shell feels comfortable. It's scary to stick our head back out of the shell. Often, what we do is stay inside, and it feels like we're doing the right thing. Unfortunately, this behavior actually strips us of power and leaves us at the mercy of our circumstances.

The first step in moving from surviving to thriving is to recognize we are in self-preservation. We have to decipher the physical signs as well as the emotional signs.

If you broke your arm, you would see a doctor who would put a cast on it. After a healing period, the cast comes off. The arm gets worked out and back to normal. Is this process painful? Yes! But it doesn't mean one must keep wearing the cast. In the same way, the mental cast is good for a time, but at some point the cast needs to come off. The person who is still healing after ten years is stuck. Imagine the infection (not to mention the muscle atrophy) keeping a cast on your arm ten years after you broke it would create! It sounds ridiculous, but counseling offices are filled with people who are stuck in a mental cast.

What are the emotional signs indicating self-preservation?

What are the physical signs indicating self-preservation?

"What is necessary to change a person is to change his awareness of himself."
Abraham Maslow

People often don't realize they are stuck in self-preservation. Here are some examples of getting stuck:

- Not being open to love because of a previous relationship.
- Not taking personal responsibility for your own part in the problem.
- Not wanting to be part of the team because of a past bad experience.
- Not making new friends because of hurt or rejection from past relationships.

What other examples can you think of?

-
-
-
-
-

Self-Growth

Moving into self-growth is where the healing process begins. We have to grieve the loss, but we also have to be willing to embrace what we have learned. Once we start looking for the life lesson in our circumstance, we become engaged—we take control of our circumstances, and we are empowered! We begin looking to the future instead of dwelling on the past. Not only are we looking to learn for ourselves, but we become willing to share our experiences with the goal of helping others. That is how this book and workbook came to exist.

Think back to some of the challenges you listed. What life lessons have you learned?

Propeller   **versus**   **Anchor**

Self-growth helps you assess your friends—whether the people in your life help you move on or keep you stuck.

It's true what they say about misery: it loves company!

Surround yourself with people who act like propellers, not anchors. Think of what an anchor does for a boat: it holds it in place and keeps it from moving. A propeller stirs the water and moves the boat forward. Anchors tell you what you *want* to hear; propellers tell you what you *need* to hear. Anchors hold you down, while propellers move you to a new place. In self-growth, it's good to take an inventory of the friends and family members who are either your propellers or anchors. Self-growth mode helps to identify the anchors in our lives and replace them with propellers.

Think of the people in your life. Who are your propellers? Who are the anchors?

Propellers	Anchors

"My best friend is the one who brings out the best in me."
3- Henry Ford

Think About It....

Are you stuck in self-preservation?

What experience have you had in the past that still holds you back?

Do you frequently discuss my crisis in a way that keeps you stuck?

Are your friends anchoring you in self-preservation, or propelling you toward self-growth?

What are you doing to move forward and grow?

Who Packed Your Parachute?

Charles Plumb, a US Naval Academy graduate, was a jet pilot in Vietnam. After 75 combat missions, his plane was destroyed by a surface-to-air missile. Plumb ejected and parachuted into enemy hands. He was captured and spent six years in a communist Vietnamese prison. He survived the ordeal and currently lectures on lessons he learned from the experience.

One day, when Plumb and his wife were sitting in a restaurant, a man at another table came up and said, "You're Plumb! You flew jet fighters in Vietnam from the aircraft carrier Kitty Hawk. You were shot down!" "How in the world did you know that?" asked Plumb. "I packed your parachute," the man replied. Plumb gasped in surprise and gratitude. The man pumped his hand and said, "I guess it worked!" Plumb assured him, "It sure did. If your chute hadn't worked, I wouldn't be here today."

That night, Plum couldn't sleep because he was thinking about the man. Plumb said, "I kept wondering what he might have looked like in a Navy uniform: a white hat, a bib in the back, and bell bottom trousers."

"I wonder how many times I might have seen him and not even said good morning, how are you, or anything because, you see, I was a fighter pilot and he was just a sailor." Plumb thought of the many hours the sailor had spent on a long wooden table in the bowels of the ship, carefully weaving the shrouds and folding the silks of each chute, holding in his hands each time the fate of someone he didn't know. Now, Plumb asks his audience, "Who's packing your parachute?" Everyone has someone who provides what they need to make it through the day. His experience reminds us all to prepare ourselves to weather whatever storms lie ahead. As you go through this week, this month, this year...recognize the people who pack your parachute.

Think About It...

Do you appreciate and acknowledge the propellers in your life?

Who are you a propeller for?

Chapter Five

Victim Versus Warrior

Our self-talk is actually linked to the behavior we decide to choose: survive or thrive. We often convince ourselves we are victims, and in our minds, we make our perceived victimization a fact. We perceive ourselves to be an innocent, helpless victim and all we can do is respond accordingly. Remember the cycle of self-talk.

Tell victim story

Create emotions/feelings of a victim

Behave like a victim

When was the last time you played the role of a victim?

When we fall into the victim role, there are actually three different types of victim stories we tell ourselves. We must be able to recognize these stories, and become willing to question the facts of the stories and also to look for other possible stories. Then, we are on the way to telling more of a warrior story and thriving.

The Three *Victim* Stories

Victim: It's not _____ fault.

Villain: It's all _____ fault.

Helpless: There's _____ I can do.

Answers on page 64

Which kind of victim story were/are you telling yourself?

What are the benefits of telling these types of stories?

One thing these stories have in common is negativity. Thinking negatively always brings people to a low point. We have to move to more positive thinking with a warrior mindset. To do this, we need to look at the attributes of a warrior story. This not only involves a conscious decision to change, but it also takes courage. Ask the following questions to come up with a more positive/warrior story.

Question Your Fictional Story

If you're telling a story where you are the *Victim*:
- Am I acting like I am an innocent sufferer?
- Am I ignoring the role that I played in contributing to the problem?
- What are my true intentions?

If you're telling a story where there is a *Villain*:
- Am I ascribing negative motives to the other person?
- Am I exaggerating my own innocence?
- Am I overemphasizing the other person's guilt?
- Am I dehumanizing the other person by making unfair generalizations?
- Am I giving excuses for my bad behavior?

If you're telling a story where you are *Helpless*:
- Am I assuming there are no alternatives to my predicament?

Do You Still Feel like a Victim?

If you still feel like a victim, or if you're unsure, read this:

"I don't want to feel this way anymore. I thought if my pain touched their lives I'd feel better. I didn't. I thought by holding it over their heads I'd feel better. I didn't. I thought by telling everyone what they'd done to me I'd feel better. I didn't; it only cost me friends and kept the pain alive. I thought if they acknowledged how wrong they've been I'd feel better. They didn't, so I felt worse. I thought if I could understand why I picked such relationships I'd feel better. So, I read books and talked with counselors. But that didn't work because I uncovered other issues I didn't have the emotional energy to deal with. I thought time would make me feel better. It helped but it didn't heal, because there were still too many things that triggered old memories. I thought after moving to a new house in a new city, and getting a new job I'd feel better. I didn't. I changed addresses but not what was going on inside me. Finally I did two things that worked; not overnight, but gradually, patiently, consistently. As I kept doing them they worked. First I decided to forgive and kept forgiving until the past no longer controlled me. Second I cried out to God, to turn me, and I shall be turned. He answered my prayer. My perception began to clear and my heart began to heal. Why? Because at last getting well meant more, so much more to me than remaining a victim. From The The Word For You Today, Alpharetta, GA 30005, Pg. 25, February 4, 2011.

Dealing with a Giant: Fear

Fear is an overwhelming emotion. Its power can cripple and paralyze its victim. The emotions power over us can seem small or large, but either way it still keeps us in survival mode. For example, a failed relationship causes you to fear the pain of another relationship, which causes you to avoid future commitments. Even the fear of disappointing someone causes us to not have a necessary conversation. The fear of what others may think often keeps us from going forward with a dream or goal. It may seem small, but we struggle against its control. Some fears can be larger than others. For an example, fear of getting on an airplane, or the fear of driving on a highway. We also encounter other fear giants that are very real such as waking up in the night convinced someone is in your room, or having a strong sense that your loved one is in trouble.

These fears fall into either of two categories:
1. Real Fear
2. False Fear

What is fear, and how does fear paralyze you?

What are examples of real fear?

-
-
-
-
-

"What torments of grief you endured, from evils that never arrived."
- Ralph Waldo Emerson

What are examples of false fear?

-
-
-
-

Why is the following statement true or not true?

"The thing you fear the most you will make come true."

Here is a helpful acronym for FEAR...

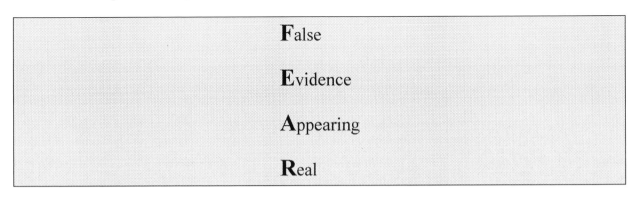

False

Evidence

Appearing

Real

What is false evidence?

How do we make false evidence appear real?

How do you harbor false fear in your heart?

What is the opposite of fear?

How do you acquire courage?

How does knowing the difference between real and false fear help you move from survive to thrive?

How do propeller friends help to diminish the effects of false fear?

How does fear affect our relationships, future and plans?

David Buell of the 8th Alabama, whose manner failed to hide the deepest anxiety he felt in battle, asked Hilary A. Herbert, "Colonel, does it occur to you that you may be killed someday in battle?" "Yes, very frequently. But why do you ask?" "Well, I thought from the fact that you never say anything about it, and then from the manner in which you expose yourself...recklessly, that you had an idea that you were in no danger of being killed." "Oh...no...I have an idea...that I am not at all exempt from any of the dangers that confront officers holding such a position as I do...I know that the probabilities are that a colonel of any infantry regiment will in all probability be either killed or seriously wounded. I have...simply made up my mind that I must take my chances...that is all there is to it."

Action Steps to Move from Victim to Warrior

1. Make the decision to change and wage war.

2. Stop negative "self-talk."

3. Develop a detailed plan complete with pros and cons.

4. Take ownership of the situation. Don't blame others.

5. Find propeller friends and create accountability.

6. Educate yourself and read positive works.

7. Count your blessings.

Your Life's Purpose

What is so valuable/important to you that you would aggressively wage war for it?

Chapter Six
Parasite Versus Player

Parasite

A parasite is an organism that grows, feeds, and is sheltered on or in a different organism, while contributing nothing to the survival of its host. In human relationships a parasite can be a metaphor for a person who habitually takes advantage of the generosity of others without making any useful return, draining the life out of everyone around them.

In 2005, when hurricane Katrina devastated New Orleans, survivors were sent to shelters as close as Texas, Louisiana, and as far away as New York. The people needed shelter, food, clothing and encouragement. Many good-natured Americans came to the rescue of their brothers and sisters, and millions of dollars in aid were raised. However, after a while, I began hearing reports of Katrina survivors who were not interested in actively helping themselves or moving on. Many started complaining because their expectations were not met. The Red Cross didn't get the money out fast enough, or the president didn't respond quickly enough. Some of the victims were even complaining about the help they were receiving. I began wondering what the people were doing to help their situation. Did they think everybody else should carry their burden? I do not intend to be insensitive to their needs; however, I believe some survivors in certain circumstances have a tendency to act more like parasites. They can attach themselves to the services of others, or feed off of the emotions of others without giving anything back.

Have you ever had a conversation with someone who loves
to talk about all the bad things happening in his or her life?

How does a conversation with this person make you feel?

Complaining is a key characteristic of parasites. The scary part is they don't realize they are complaining! It can be very difficult to identify this behavior in ourselves. Once complaining becomes a habit, it is challenging to undo it. Like a parasite, it drains you and everyone you come in contact with of energy and joy!

Think About It...

Think about your conversations over the last few days.

How many times could statements you made be called complaints?

What kind of things did you complain about?

Why do we complain?

What is the benefit for us?

"When you blame others, you give up your power to change."
Dr. Robert Anthony

Player

Players, unlike parasites who sit on the sidelines and whine about losing, get into the game and do their part to win. Players choose to step up to the plate and swing the bat. If they miss the ball, they keep at it until they eventually connect.

The following are some of the key differences between parasites and players.

1. *Players constructively discuss the issues in their lives instead of complaining.*

Think about some of the complaints you listed above. How could you change complaints to discussions?

2. *Players are willing to take the risk of changing from a parasite to a player.*

What are the risks involved in deciding to move to a thriving Player?

3. *Players develop a mental discipline to stay focused on their goals and dreams.*

Players don't let negative comments, critiques, or opinions get them off track.

Players understand how important it is to have a strong mental focus.

The Tiny Frog Competition

Once upon a time, there was a bunch of tiny frogs who arranged a running competition among themselves. The goal was to reach the top of a very high tower. A huge crowd gathered around the tower to see the race and cheer on the contestants. The race began.

No one in the crowd really believed that the tiny frogs could reach the top of the tower. "Oh, it's way too difficult!!" The crowd said. "They will never make it to the top." "There is not a chance they will succeed because the tower is too high!"

The tiny frogs began collapsing, one by one—except for those who, in a fresh tempo, were climbing higher and higher.

The crowd continued to yell, "It is just too difficult. No one will make it!"

More tiny frogs got tired and gave up. But, one continued higher and higher. At the end, everyone else had given up climbing the tower except for one tiny frog who, after a big effort, was the only one who reached the top!

All of the other tiny frogs naturally wanted to know how this one frog managed to do it. A contestant asked the winner how he had found the strength to succeed and reach the goal.

The winner couldn't answer because he couldn't hear the question. He was deaf!

How can people develop mental discipline?

4. *Players rely on spiritual fitness.*

Spiritual fitness is equally important in a player mindset. Beliefs are the foundation of how we live our lives. Beliefs help us answer the deeper questions like:

Who am I? Why am I here? What is my purpose? These are the key questions we ask when life gets us down. When we don't have a belief system or lose sight of our existing beliefs, we set ourselves up to get stuck in survival mode. It's like trying to drive a car without a steering wheel; we aren't going to get very far.

What we believe is critical to move from a survive mode to a thriving mode. Our belief systems can be very different, but one thing is for certain: beliefs are foundational to our desires and ability to move ahead.

How strong is your foundation? What are your beliefs? What do you do to stay connected with them, nourish, and strengthen them?

5. *Players make the call.*

Players don't wait for someone else to make things happen. They take the necessary action to make decisions instead of waiting for something or someone else to do it for them. Players don't wait and hope things will get better. They come up with a plan, implement the plan and make things happen. Players take control of their lives. What barriers keep you from taking control and making the call?

6. *Players have a Kemosabe.*

Remember Tonto and the Lone Ranger? It was a popular TV show many years ago. Tonto always greeted the Lone Ranger by addressing him as "Kemosabe." The origin of this expression is somewhat unclear, but James Jewell (an early director of the radio series) said the name originated from a boy's camp located on Mullett Lake, Michigan, that his father-in-law directed from 1911 to 1941. The translation meant "trusty scout," which Tonto explains in the pilot of the Clayton Moore TV series, *Enter the Lone Ranger*. Fran Striker, the writer of *The Lone Ranger* scripts, also said the actual expression was Ta-i ke-mo sah-bee, which he said meant "Greetings, trusty scout."

Over time, the phrase "faithful friend" has also been associated with the term Kemosabe. The Lone Ranger was the person Tonto looked to for answers to difficult situations.

We talked earlier about propellers and anchors. It is critical, especially during tough times that we are close to our propellers and Kemosabes!

Chapter Seven

Actor Versus Director

Actor

An actor is someone who works in a play, movie, or TV show. They portray a character for the enjoyment and entertainment of an audience. Their performance involves memorizing lines, calling up emotions, and knowing the proper time to deliver the material. When we are in survival mode, we have a tendency to become actors. Actors in survival mode need direction from something outside of themselves. Often, they wait on someone else to show them their part. They need someone to give them direction and focus. Many times we behave like actors when we don't feel very confident.

There are times in our lives when taking on the role of an actor is necessary. We must listen to, and heed the advice of others who are wise and more experienced. Acting is not always a bad thing. In certain seasons, we need the direction of others. However, there are some negative aspects of being an actor, especially when we cling to the actor role for too long, and refuse to become the directors of our lives. We behave like *surviving* actors when we:

- **Take direction from outside, not inside.** When we are in survival mode, we tend not to see what course our decisions could take. Similar to actors who need to be coached on these decisions to be sure they are seeing things clearly. There are times when we need direction and help from others who see the facts and realities we may not see. Again, it's not bad to take direction from others when you are surviving a crisis. However, transitioning into a thriving life requires you to become the director.

- **Live for the applause of others.** Actors live for the attention of others. The attention and sympathy we get from others who hear our survivor stories is addictive. Giving in to the desire to talk about our past hurts excessively, and receiving outside attention can take hold of us, and own us, similar to a drug addiction. If we are not careful, we can re-live the past in order to feed our addictive need for attention. This thirst for sympathy and attention can keep us stuck in survival mode.

- **Act like someone else.** Actors on stage assume the personality of the character they are pretending to be; the person they want you to see. However, nobody gets to know the real person inside. Survivor-actors tend to be closed and introverted. When in survival mode, our emotions about the situation can be so vivid that we are uncertain who we are. This causes us to be unsure about our decisions, and we tend to second-guess the choices we do make.

- **Base their confidence on what others think of them.** All of us struggle with rejection on some level. However, moving forward into a thrive mode means you may need to stand alone with your decision, and that's OK. You know you are transitioning from a survivor to thrive mode when you feel confident about your decisions and can stand behind them.

- **Act on cue:** Just as "Lights, camera, action!" is a key command from the director on a movie set, we could be waiting for our cue to act or move toward some kind of action, or for someone to tell us what to do. Actors will perform on cue when given direction. When in survival mode, we are often waiting on direction from someone else because we are not sure we can trust our own decisions.

Director

In contrast to actors, thrivers are more apt to take charge and direct their own lives.

Taking responsibility and ownership in your situation is the essence of being a thriver and a director. Directing is about taking credit for the things we do right and owning up to the things that don't go right, rather than shifting ownership elsewhere. When we are directors, we deal with our lives scene by scene, so we never losing the vision of the total picture.

Thrivers behave as directors when they:

- **Take the script and improve it**. Instead of wishing for a different "life script," directors take the one that's given to them and improve it as they go.

- **Listen to what is in their heart in addition to outside advice.** Directors need propeller friends and the ability to listen to their advice. But, remember sometimes friends' suggestions are made with a bias view of the situation. Seek the counsel of others, but also listen to your instincts.

- **Don't wait around for other people to bring them success.** Directors don't wait for success. They create it. Some people believe people around them are luckier than themselves. Alternatively, directors understand that most luck is actually due to persistence and endurance. Their success comes through hard work and diligence. Directors do not waiting around for success to find them.

- **Become the boss when on the set.** Directors understand that they have ownership over their decisions, attitudes, and actions. They are their own boss, and are accountable for what they create. There is a distinct difference between meeting an actor, and the director of a play. You know the director is in charge by the way he or she takes control of a situation. Directors let people know they have a vision and a direction.

- **Deal with the critics.** Critics are everywhere. Try doing something great, and soon you'll find a heckler in the crowd. Actors are devastated when the critics attack them; directors understand not everyone will agree with their approach. Even still, they have a strong sense of self with the ability to stay focused on their goal.

- **Have a vision of what they want their life to look like.** Directors have a vision for the life they want. If you ask them about it, they will have a clear direction and purpose. They tend to be goal-oriented and work hard to achieve these goals despite the challenges. Their picture of their goals keeps them focused and keeps them going.

Think About It...

Are you more of an actor or director?

Am I confident about my opinions, visions and dreams?
Or, am I acting out someone else's plan for me?

Do I write my life script or just take the one I feel life hands me and respond?

How am I taking my life script and making it better?

How do I react to my critics?

Chapter Eight

Thriving Is a Learned Behavior

How do you learn to thrive? Practice, practice, practice!

The following are seven signs that you've moved from surviving to thriving.

1. *Thankfulness* – **You are grateful for your life and believe there's a point in it all.** Even though you've faced the darkness, you can still embrace the light.

"You cannot be grateful and bitter.
You cannot be grateful and unhappy.
You cannot be grateful and without hope.
You cannot be grateful and unloving.
So just be grateful."
Author Unknown

Is your focus on what you have, or what you don't have?

At the end of the day, do you take time to count your blessings?

Now, make a list of what you have to be grateful for:

1.

2.

3.

4.

5.

2. *Humor* – **You're laughing.** Humor is a powerful tool. It turns us around and keeps things in balance when life seems unfair. It's also an easy way to strengthen the heart muscle. Twenty seconds of laughter can equal three minutes of strenuous exercise.

3. *Release* – **You can let go of the past.** You have your feelings, but you don't let your feelings have you. You let go of bad things when they are over and argue effectively against your self-defeating thoughts.

Think About It...

What are you holding onto from your past?

What do you have to do to let go and move on?

---

4. *Influence* – **You respond appropriately when the heat is on.** Remember the egg, coffee bean and carrot illustration from earlier? Rather than wilting in the face of adversity or hardening your heart, release a part of yourself to influence your situation, touching others with your richness of spirit. **People are watching you and your response.**

5. *Vision* – **You can envision the possible.** You use your imagination to enhance the quality of your life now. You dream big and invest your time and energy into creating a way to make your goals come true. The perspective is found in the age-old question, "Is the glass half-full, or is it half empty?" Half-empty glasses bring half-empty results, while a positive outlook can fill up the world with new possibilities.

What are the visions for your life?

1.

2.

3.

6. *Encouragement* – **You surround yourself with a supportive team.** You realize you can't do life alone, and invite people into your life who love and support you at every turn. Be sure you have propeller friends. The kind of people who can help you move forward and focus on your options, and become a part of a support team for others. Let others know you are there to help them get to the top of the mountain. You will grow through these experiences, and create lifelong friends.

7. *Responsibility* – **You're making things happen.** Rather than lamenting your plight, you're putting one foot in front of the other and getting on with your life. You've turned adversity to your advantage with a more aware, appreciative, and ardent involvement in the activities of daily life.

How do you create accountability?

	Surviving			Thriving
1.	**Self-Preservation**	vs.		**Self-Growth**
	Shocked			Healing
	Withdrawn			Engaged
	Helpless			Empowered
2.	**Victim**	vs.		**Warrior**
	Blaming			Accountable
	Hopeless			Determined
	Emotional			Logical
3.	**Parasite**	vs.		**Player**
	Passive			Assertive
	Energy-absorbing			Energy-producing
	Reactive			Proactive
4.	**Actor**	vs.		**Director**
	Can't be done			Can be done
	Present-focused			Future-focused
	Unclear identity			Clear identity

"A ship in harbor is safe, but that is not what ships are built for."
John A. Shedd

Answer Keys

Answers to *Fact or Fiction?* (Page 16)

1. Fact
2. Fiction
3. Fact
4. Fiction
5. Fiction
6. Fiction
7. Fiction
8. Fact
9. Fiction
10. Fact
11. Fiction
12. Fact

Answers to *The Three Victim Stories* (Page 35)

Victim: It's not **my** fault.

Villain: It's all **your** fault

Helpless: There's **nothing** I can do.

About the Authors

Stepp Stevens Sydnor

Stepp has twenty-four years of experience in working with startup and established organizations to turn around their businesses. He is also a lifelong student of human behavior from both the psychological and spiritual perspective. The synergy between his business experiences and his understanding of human behavior has brought a uniquely integrated perspective to his business and his coaching.

    In 1999, Stepp founded The TurnAround Group, now TurnAround Training Solutions, LLC, to help companies improve their profitability by focusing on their employees. He has developed training, coaching and mentoring programs in the areas of sales, leadership, culture, personal development and stress management. Clients have ranged from public-sector organizations such as PricewaterhouseCoopers and Dallas Housing Authority to industry leaders such as Cox Communications, Sam's Club, Time Warner Cable and Robroy Industries.

    An accomplished speaker, Stepp conducts seminars regularly for corporations and other organizations. He is the father of three teenagers.

Suzi Streit

Suzi is a trainer, coach and motivational speaker with TurnAround Solutions. She works with TurnAround Solutions CEO Stepp Stevens Sydnor to deliver dynamic leadership, communication and team-building programs to the business community. She also provides one-on-one training that ensures tools learned in training become life habits.

    Before joining TurnAround Solutions, Suzi worked for ten years as a certified instructor with the Dale Carnegie Program. Her skills in human dynamics have been the foundation of her work with TurnAround Solutions. She teaches a wide range of courses designed to improve leadership skills and enhance professional and personal interactions—from *Crucial Conversations*® by VitalSmarts™, for which she is a certified instructor, to DiSC Style Analysis™. Suzi has also developed several of TurnAround Solutions' innovative, interactive training curriculums, from time management to coaching style management.

    Suzi has a degree in business administration from Stephen F. Austin State University. She and her husband, Brad, are the parents of two sons.

For more information on how you can launch into a more thriving life, please contact us at:

> **TurnAround Training Solutions, LLC**
> Marketing Department
> P.O. Box 10111
> Tyler, TX 75711
> 903-533-0591
> E-mail: getthecure@turnaroundsolutions.net
> Website: www.turnaroundsolutions.net

Do you have an inspiring surviving-to-thriving story? Please e-mail it to us. We would love to see how this study has helped shape the events of your life.

Other Training from TurnAround Solutions

Communication skills development

Conflict Resolution

Coaching Style Leadership training

Create Opportunity for Selling, Prospecting and Networking

Managing Salespeople

Corporate Culture

Customer Service

Hiring and Employee Development Assessment Tools

Endnote

---

[i] **Chapter 1: No One Said Life Is Fair**

Berit Kjos, *A Wardrobe from the King* (Wheaton, IL: Victor Books, 1988) 45-46, www.crossroad.to.